TABLE OF CONTENTS

JOKES AND RIDDLES
3

KNOCK KNOCK JOKES
44

WRITE YOUR OWN JOKES
49

Copyright © 2019 Sarah Ritter

All rights reserved.

ISBN: 9781079342284

JOKES And RIDDLES

~

WHAT KIND OF TREE FITS IN YOUR HAND?

A palm tree!

~

WHY IS CINDERELLA SO BAD AT SOCCER?

Because she always runs away from the ball!

~

WHAT DID THE LEFT EYE SAY TO THE RIGHT EYE?

Between us, something smells!

~

~

WHY DID THE TEDDY BEARS SAY NO TO DESSERT?

Because they were stuffed.

~

WHERE DO POLAR BEARS KEEP THEIR MONEY?

In a snow bank!

~

WHEN WILL THE LITTLE SNAKE ARRIVE?

I don't know, but he won't be long.

~

~

WHAT DO YOU CALL A DINOSAUR THAT IS SLEEPING?

A dino-snore!

~

WHAT IS FAST, LOUD AND CRUNCHY?

A rocket chip!

~

HOW DO YOU GET A SQUIRREL TO LIKE YOU?

Act like a nut!

~

~

WHY DID THE DINOSAUR REFUSE TO WEAR DEODORANT?

He didn't want to be ex-stink.

~

WHAT HAS EARS BUT CANNOT HEAR?

A cornfield.

~

WHAT DID ONE PLATE SAY TO THE OTHER PLATE?

Dinner is on me!

~

WHAT DO YOU GET WHEN YOU CROSS A VAMPIRE AND A SNOWMAN?

Frost bite!

~

WHY DID THE STUDENT EAT HIS HOMEWORK?

Because the teacher told him it was a piece of cake!

~

WHEN YOU LOOK FOR SOMETHING, WHY IS IT ALWAYS IN THE LAST PLACE YOU LOOK?

Because when you find it, you stop looking.

~

WHAT IS BROWN, HAIRY AND WEARS SUNGLASSES?

A coconut at the beach.

~

WHAT KIND OF WATER CANNOT FREEZE?

Hot water.

~

A PICKLE WAS COMPLAINING TO ANOTHER PICKLE. WHAT DID ONE SAY TO THE OTHER?

Just dill with it.

~

WHAT DID THE DALMATIAN SAY AFTER LUNCH?

That hit the spot!

~

WHY DID THE KIDS CROSS THE PLAYGROUND?

To get to the other slide.

~

WHAT ANIMAL IS ALWAYS AT A BASEBALL GAME?

A bat.

~

~

HOW DOES A VAMPIRE START A LETTER?

Tomb it may concern...

~

HOW DO YOU STOP AN ASTRONAUT'S BABY FROM CRYING?

You rocket!

~

WHY WAS 6 AFRAID OF 7?

Because 7, 8, 9

~

~

WHAT IS A WITCH'S FAVORITE SUBJECT IN SCHOOL?

Spelling!

~

HOW DO YOU MAKE A LEMON DROP?

Just let it fall.

~

WHAT DID THE LIMESTONE SAY TO THE GEOLOGIST?

Don't take me for granite!

~

~

WHAT DO YOU CALL A DUCK THAT GETS ALL A'S?

A wise quacker.

~

WHY DOES A SEAGULL FLY OVER THE SEA?

Because if it flew over the bay, it would be a baygull!

~

WHY DID THE PONY GET SENT TO HIS ROOM?

He wouldn't stop horsing around.

~

~

WHY DID THE COOKIE GO TO THE HOSPITAL?

Because he felt crummy.

~

WHY WAS THE BABY STRAWBERRY CRYING?

Because her mom and dad were in a jam.

~

WHAT DID THE LITTLE CORN SAY TO THE MAMA CORN?

Where is Pop corn?

~

HOW MUCH DOES IT COST A PIRATE TO GET HIS EARS PIERCED?

About a buck an ear.

~

WHERE WOULD YOU FIND AN ELEPHANT?

The same place you lost her!

~

HOW DO YOU TALK TO A GIANT?

Use big words!

~

~

WHAT FALLS IN WINTER BUT NEVER GETS HURT?

Snow!

~

WHAT DO YOU CALL A GHOST'S TRUE LOVE?

His ghoul-friend.

~

WHAT BUILDING IN NEW YORK HAS THE MOST STORIES?

The public library!

~

~

WHAT DID ONE VOLCANO SAY TO THE OTHER?

I lava you!

~

HOW DO WE KNOW THAT THE OCEAN IS FRIENDLY?

It waves!

~

WHAT IS A TORNADO'S FAVORITE GAME TO PLAY?

Twister!

~

~

WHAT DO YOU CALL TWO BIRDS IN LOVE?

Tweethearts!

HOW DOES A SCIENTIST FRESHEN HER BREATH?

With experi-mints!

~

HOW ARE FALSE TEETH LIKE STARS?

They come out at night!

~

HOW CAN YOU TELL A VAMPIRE HAS A COLD?

She starts coffin.

~

WHAT'S WORSE THAN FINDING A WORM IN YOUR APPLE?

Finding half a worm.

~

WHAT IS A COMPUTER'S FAVORITE SNACK?

Computer chips!

~

WHAT WAS THE FIRST ANIMAL IN SPACE?

The cow that jumped over the moon

~

~

WHAT DID THE APPLE SAY TO THE DOG?

Nothing. Apples can't talk.

~

WHAT TIME IS IT WHEN THE CLOCK STRIKES 13?

Time to get a new clock.

~

HOW DOES A CUCUMBER BECOME A PICKLE?

It goes through a jarring experience.

~

WHAT DO YOU CALL A BOOMERANG THAT WON'T COME BACK?

A stick.

~

WHAT DO YOU THINK OF THAT NEW DINER ON THE MOON?

Food was good, but there really wasn't much atmosphere.

~

HOW DO YOU MAKE A TISSUE DANCE?

You put a little boogie in it.

~

WHAT DID THE NOSE SAY TO THE FINGER?

Quit picking on me!

~

WHAT MUSICAL INSTRUMENT IS FOUND IN THE BATHROOM?

A tuba toothpaste.

~

WHY DID THE KID BRING A LADDER TO SCHOOL?

Because she wanted to go to high school.

~

WHAT IS A VAMPIRE'S FAVORITE FRUIT?

A blood orange.

~

WHAT DO ELVES LEARN IN SCHOOL?

The elf-abet.

~

WHAT DO YOU CALL A DOG MAGICIAN?

A Labracadabrador.

~

WHERE DO PENCILS GO ON VACATION?

Pencil-vania.

~

WHY COULDN'T THE PONY SING A LULLABY?

She was a little hoarse.

~

WHY DIDN'T THE SKELETON GO TO THE DANCE?

He had no body to dance with.

~

WHY DID THE BANANA GO TO THE DOCTOR?

Because it wasn't peeling well.

~

~

WHAT DO YOU CALL A FAKE NOODLE?

An impasta.

~

WHAT STAYS IN THE CORNER YET CAN TRAVEL ALL OVER THE WORLD?

A stamp.

~

HOW DO YOU FIX A CRACKED PUMPKIN?

With a pumpkin patch.

~

WHAT KIND OF AWARD DID THE DENTIST RECEIVE?

A little plaque.

~

WHAT DO YOU CALL A FUNNY MOUNTAIN?

Hill-arious.

~

WHY ARE GHOSTS BAD LIARS?

Because you can see right through them.

~

WHY DO BEES HAVE STICKY HAIR?

Because they use a honeycomb.

~

WHAT DID THE BIG FLOWER SAY TO THE LITTLE FLOWER?

Hi, bud!

~

WHAT DID THE ASTRONAUT SAY WHEN HE CRASHED INTO THE MOON?

"I Apollo-gize."

~

WHY DIDN'T THE ORANGE WIN THE RACE?

It ran out of juice.

~

WHAT DINOSAUR HAD THE BEST VOCABULARY?

The thesaurus.

~

WHAT DID ONE DNA STRAND SAY TO THE OTHER DNA STRAND?

Do these genes make my butt look big?

~

WHY AREN'T DOGS GOOD DANCERS?

They have two left feet.

~

WHY DID JOHNNY THROW THE CLOCK OUT OF THE WINDOW?

Because he wanted to see time fly.

~

WHAT DID ONE TOILET SAY TO THE OTHER?

You look flushed.

~

WHY DID THE MAN PUT HIS MONEY IN THE FREEZER?

He wanted cold hard cash!

~

~

WHY COULDN'T THE ASTRONAUT BOOK A HOTEL ON THE MOON?

Because it was full.

~

WHAT DID THE FINGER SAY TO THE THUMB?

I'm in glove with you!

~

HOW DO PICKLES ENJOY A DAY OUT?

They relish it.

~

WHAT DO YOU CALL A HOT SNOWMAN?

Water.

~

WHAT'S A PIRATE'S FAVORITE LETTER?

Arrrrrrrrrr!

~

WHAT DO YOU GET WHEN YOU CROSS AN ELEPHANT WITH A FISH?

Swimming trunks.

~

HOW DO YOU THROW A PARTY IN SPACE?

You planet.

WHAT HAPPENED WHEN THE SKUNK WAS ON TRIAL?

The judge declared, "Odor in the court, odor in the court!"

~

WHAT DO YOU CALL A SLEEPING BULL?

A bulldozer!

~

WHY DID THE TOMATO BLUSH?

It saw the salad dressing.

~

~

WHAT DO YOU GET WHEN YOU CROSS A CENTIPEDE WITH A PARROT?

A walkie talkie.

~

WHY ARE ROBOTS NEVER AFRAID?

They have nerves of steel.

~

WHY DID THE CABBAGE WIN THE RACE?

Because it was a-head.

~

~

WHAT DOES A BOOK DO IN THE WINTER?

It wears a jacket.

~

WHAT KIND OF HAIRCUTS TO BEES GET?

Buzzzzzcuts.

~

WHAT DO YOU GET IF YOU CROSS A PIE AND A SNAKE?

A pie-thon.

~

WHY DIDN'T THE ROBOT FINISH HIS BREAKFAST?

Because the orange juice told him to concentrate.

~

WHY CAN'T YOU PLAY SPORTS WITH PIGS?

They always hog the ball.

~

WHY DO PORCUPINES ALWAYS WIN THE GAME?

They have the most points.

~

WHERE DO ELEPHANTS PACK THEIR CLOTHES?

In their trunks!

~

WHAT DOES BREAD DO ON VACATION?

Loaf around.

~

WHY WAS THE BROOM RUNNING LATE?

It over-swept.

~

WHAT PART OF THE FISH WEIGHS THE MOST?

The scales.

~

WHAT DO GHOSTS LIKE TO EAT IN THE SUMMER?

I Scream.

~

WHY DID THE TEACHER WEAR SUNGLASSES TO SCHOOL?

Because her students were so bright.

~

WHAT DID ONE TOILET SAY TO THE OTHER?

You look a bit flushed!

~

WHERE DO SHEEP GO ON VACATION?

The Baaa-hamas.

~

WHAT DOES EVERY BIRTHDAY END WITH?

The letter Y.

~

WHY DO BIRDS FLY?

It's faster than walking.

~

WHY DID SUPERMAN FLUSH THE TOILET?

Because it was his doody.

~

CAN FEBRUARY MARCH?

No, but April May.

~

WHAT TIME DO DUCKS WAKE UP?

At the quack of dawn.

~

WHY DID THE GIRAFFES GET BAD GRADES?

She had her head in the clouds.

~

WHAT DID THE FLOWER SAY AFTER IT TOLD A JOKE?

I was just pollen your leg.

~

WHO DID THE ZOMBIE TAKE TO THE PROM?

His ghoul-friend!

~

WHAT DID THE TRAFFIC LIGHT SAY TO THE TRUCK?

Don't look, I'm changing.

~

WHY DIDN'T THE ZOMBIE GO TO SCHOOL?

He felt rotten!

~

WHAT DOES A CLOUD WEAR?

Thunderwear!

~

WHY DIDN'T THE KOALA BEAR GET THE JOB?

They said she was over-koala-fied.

~

WHAT DO YOU CALL AN OWL MAGICIAN?

Who-dini.

~

WHAT KIND OF VEGETABLE IS ANGRY?

A steamed carrot!

~

WHY ISN'T THERE A CLOCK IN THE LIBRARY?

Because it tocks too much.

~

WHAT DAY OF THE WEEK ARE MOST TWINS BORN ON?

Twos-day!

~

~

WHY DO MATH BOOKS ALWAYS LOOK SO SAD?

They are full of problems.

~

HOW DOES THE OCEAN SAY HELLO?

It waves.

KNOCK KNOCK JOKES

Knock! Knock!

Who's there?

Wooden shoe.

Wooden shoe who?

Wooden shoe like to hear another joke?

~

Knock! Knock!

Who's there?

Boo.

Boo who?

Don't cry, it's just me!

Knock! Knock!

Who's there?

Justin.

Justin who?

Justin time for dinner!

~

Knock! Knock!

Who's there?

Beats.

Beats who?

Beats me.

Knock! Knock!

Who's there?

Cow says.

Cow says who?

No, silly! A cow says "Mooooo!"

~

Knock! Knock!

Who's there?

Owls say.

Owls say who?

Yes, they do.

Knock! Knock!
Who's there?
Little old lady.
Little old lady who?
I didn't know you could yodel.

~

Knock! Knock!
Who's there?
Spell.
Spell who?
W-H-O.

WRITE YOUR OWN JOKES

Write down your own jokes here! Be creative and have fun!

Made in the USA
Lexington, KY
31 August 2019